A Gift For

_____

From

_____

STRENGTH *for the* SOUL *from* OUR DAILY BREAD

Grief

Discovery House Publishers

Books, music, and videos that feed the soul with the Word of God

Box 3566 Grand Rapids, MI 49501

Discovery House Publishers is affiliated with RBC Ministries,
Grand Rapids, Michigan.

Discovery House books are distributed to the trade exclusively by
Barbour Publishing, Inc., Uhrichsville, Ohio.

Requests for permission to quote from this book should be
directed to Permissions Department, Discovery House
Publishers, P.O. Box 3566, Grand Rapids, MI 49501.

Interior design by Sherri L. Hoffman

Printed in Italy
06 07 08 09 / L.E.G.O. / 10 9 8 7 6 5 4 3 2 1

Introduction

*S*ince April 1956, millions of readers around the world have found daily inspiration, help, comfort, and biblical truth from the pages of *Our Daily Bread*. Now you can find comfort from one of the most beloved devotionals on the subject of grief, compiled into one convenient volume.

We hope that this book will be of help to you and those you know in times of grief, sorrow, and loss. May it and the Word of God bring strength to your soul.

Other books in the Strength for the Soul
from *Our Daily Bread* series

Comfort
Hope
Peace
Prayer
Trust

Valley of the Shadow

The LORD is my shepherd, I shall not be in want.
   He makes me lie down in green pastures,
he leads me beside quiet waters,
   he restores my soul.
He guides me in paths of righteousness
   for his name's sake.
Even though I walk
   through the valley of the shadow of death,
I will fear no evil,
   for you are with me;
your rod and your staff,
   they comfort me.   —PSALM 23:1–4

*D*arkness upon darkness. Sorrow upon sorrow. Pain upon pain. Anguish upon anguish. That's death.

Death is a fearful visitor, snatching away people who are precious to us and leaving us behind to mourn, grieve, and wonder. It blocks the light that before had shined so freely and easily on our lives.

Whether we're facing the prospect of dying, or dealing with the death of a loved one, death can be devastating. It can sap our energy, change our plans, overwhelm our soul, alter our outlook, test our faith, steal our joy, and challenge our assumptions about life's purposes.

When we walk through the deep valley, we feel swallowed up by the shadow and come face-to-face with fear. The frantic emptiness of our loss threatens the comfort that previously originated from our trust in God, and so we grow afraid. Afraid of our future. Afraid to enjoy life again.

Yet in that valley, under that shadow, we can say to the Lord, "I will fear no evil; for you are with me" (Psalm 23:4). His loving arms never let us go. He is always with us.

Slowly at first, but most assuredly, He provides comfort and release from the darkness. He gives light. He leads us out. Eventually, we escape the valley of the shadow.   —DAVE BRANON

Better Than Words

"Behold, my eye has seen all this,
    My ear has heard and understood it.
What you know, I also know;
    I am not inferior to you.
But I would speak to the Almighty,
    And I desire to reason with God.
But you forgers of lies,
    You are all worthless physicians.
Oh, that you would be silent,
    And it would be your wisdom!

—JOB 13:1-5 (NKJV)

When we are with people who are grieving or suffering, we may feel a need to fill the awkwardness of the occasion with words. Not to say something, we fear, is to let them down. We may even find ourselves avoiding the bereaved because we're afraid we won't know what to say.

Author Joe Bayly, who lost three sons through death, described two examples of comfort he received during his deepest grief:

> Someone came and talked to me of God's dealings, of why it happened, of hope beyond the grave. He talked constantly [and] said things I knew were true. I was unmoved, except to wish he'd go away. He finally did.
>
> Another came and sat beside me. He didn't talk. He didn't ask leading questions. He just sat beside me for an hour and more, listened when I said something, answered briefly, prayed simply, [and] left. I was moved. I was comforted. I hated to see him go.

Job experienced similar emotions. In his grief, he too had craved silent support from his friends. He cried out, "Oh, that you would be silent, and it would be your wisdom!" (13:5). Instead, he was worn down by their many words.

The next time you're with people who are grieving, allow your presence to be their comfort.   —JOANIE YODER

Handling a Great Sorrow

The king was shaken. He went up to the room over the gateway and wept. As he went, he said: "O my son Absalom! My son, my son Absalom! If only I had died instead of you—O Absalom, my son, my son!" . . .

Then Joab went into the house to the king and said, "Today you have humiliated all your men, who have just saved your life and the lives of your sons and daughters and the lives of your wives and concubines. You love those who hate you and hate those who love you. You have made it clear today that the commanders and their men mean nothing to you. I see that you would be pleased if Absalom were alive today and all of us were dead. Now go out and encourage your men. I swear by the LORD that if you don't go out, not a man will be left with you by nightfall. This will be worse for you than all the calamities that have come upon you from your youth till now."

So the king got up and took his seat in the gateway. When the men were told, "The king is sitting in the gateway," they all came before him. —2 SAMUEL 18:33; 19:5–8

*P*eople often react foolishly when overwhelmed by sorrow. For example, a young woman whose husband was killed in war became so bitter that she started having affairs with married men, disrupting their homes and breaking many hearts. David was so crushed by grief at the death of his son Absalom that he temporarily forgot his responsibility as God's anointed king of Israel.

Christians, however, should not allow grief to plunge them into despair, for they can use their sorrow to accomplish much for the Lord. When David heeded the rebuke of Joab, recorded in 2 Samuel 19:5–8, he gained a more loyal and devoted following than he had enjoyed before the revolt of his son.

Another example of how to react to bereavement is Dwight L. Moody, who was deeply saddened by the unexpected death of his beloved brother Sam. To carry out Sam's dream of founding a Bible training school for girls dressed "not in velvet but in calico," the evangelist threw his energies and enthusiasm into the project, which was completed at Northfield, Massachusetts, in 1879.

Sorrows are inevitable, and avoiding them should not be the goal of our petitions. Instead, we ought to prepare ourselves, so that when grief comes, it will not make us bitter and paralyze us into uselessness. If we humbly walk with God in prayer and obedience to His Word, we will find the strength to turn great losses into stepping-stones to spiritual achievements, and to become more effective witnesses for Christ. By God's grace determine that you will handle your sorrows wisely and not let them handle you!   —HERB VANDER LUGT

"Mother, I Heard That!"

Soon afterward, Jesus went to a town called Nain, and his disciples and a large crowd went along with him. As he approached the town gate, a dead person was being carried out—the only son of his mother, and she was a widow. And a large crowd from the town was with her. When the Lord saw her, his heart went out to her and he said, "Don't cry."

Then he went up and touched the coffin, and those carrying it stood still. He said, "Young man, I say to you, get up!" The dead man sat up and began to talk, and Jesus gave him back to his mother. —LUKE 7:11–15

*L*uke 7 pictures for us the touching scene of a grief-stricken widow taking her only son to be buried. Her sorrow is almost more than she can bear. Death had already claimed her husband, and now has laid its chilling hand on her one remaining relative. W. P. Siebert gives this description:

> The long walk to the cemetery has begun. Finally the procession reaches the city gates. Soon her loved one will be removed from her sight forever. Then the mourners meet a group of men. One of them speaks to the widow and tells her not to weep. The words of this Man ring with such a note of authority that her sobbing is replaced by a tranquil peace. This compassionate One halts those who bear her son's body and addresses the corpse, "Young man, I say unto thee, Arise." To the amazement of all, "he that was dead sat up, and began to speak."

Another commentator imagines this widow of Nain talking that night with her resurrected son. "When our friends and I were following your coffin to the burial place, Jesus the Messiah met us. He stopped our procession and said, 'Weep not.' Then touching your casket, He looked at you and said, 'Young man, I say unto thee, Arise.'" "Mother, I heard that!" exclaimed the happy youth. "You don't have to say any more. I know the rest!"

This same Jesus still sympathizes with His sorrowing children and tells us not to weep, for someday our loved ones too "will hear His voice and come forth" (John 5:28–29).

—Henry Bosch

Good Grieving

When Mary reached the place where Jesus was and saw him, she fell at his feet and said, "Lord, if you had been here, my brother would not have died."

When Jesus saw her weeping, and the Jews who had come along with her also weeping, he was deeply moved in spirit and troubled. "Where have you laid him?" he asked. "Come and see, Lord," they replied.

Jesus wept. . . . Then the Jews said, "See how he loved him!"

—JOHN 11:32–36

In his book *Good Grief*, Granger Westburg points out that any significant loss in life can throw a person into a state of grief. It may be the death of a loved one, separation through divorce, a job termination, or even the death of a child's pet. If the strong feelings associated with such experiences are recognized as normal and do not lead to withdrawal from life, grief can be good. To hold these emotions back, however, can spell trouble.

A Christian periodical told of a mother who witnessed her son's death in an automobile accident. The well-meaning members of her church told her to "be brave" and not to express her feelings. They said it just "wasn't Christian" to sorrow. So she bottled up her tears inside. This led to a nervous breakdown. To add to her heartache, those same people chided her with, "How can a Christian have a nervous breakdown?"

This may be an extreme case, yet it reflects a widespread misconception about tragedy and tears. Robots can remain impassive when they are torn apart inside—but not people. We are equipped with tear ducts, designed and created by God, to serve as outlets for the strong emotions brought on by life's crises.

Mary and Martha were not ashamed to cry or talk out their feelings. They were in touch with their emotions. Even more significant, Jesus Himself wept when He saw the pain caused by sin and death. But His raising of Lazarus from the grave demonstrated that sadness could be turned into gladness. He welcomes our tears so that He can wipe them away.

—DENNIS DE HAAN

15

Why Cry?

"O Jerusalem, Jerusalem, you who kill the prophets and stone those sent to you, how often I have longed to gather your children together, as a hen gathers her chicks under her wings, but you were not willing!

Look, your house is left to you desolate. I tell you, you will not see me again until you say, 'Blessed is he who comes in the name of the Lord.'" . . .

Jesus turned and said to them, "Daughters of Jerusalem, do not weep for me; weep for yourselves and for your children. For the time will come when you will say, 'Blessed are the barren women, the wombs that never bore and the breasts that never nursed!' Then 'they will say to the mountains, "Fall on us!" and to the hills, "Cover us!"' For if men do these things when the tree is green, what will happen when it is dry?"

—LUKE 13:34–35; 23:28–31

*T*ears are stronger than words and more binding than treaties. In 1947, President Harry S. Truman visited Chapaltepec Castle, the West Point of Mexico. A hundred years earlier, when US troops had captured the citadel, six cadets had been the only survivors, and they had all committed suicide rather than surrender. As Truman placed a wreath on the monument to the heroes and bowed his head, the cadets in the color guard burst into tears. Someone said that nothing did more to help cement the two countries together than the emotion expressed on that occasion.

The Christian, indwelt by the Holy Spirit, can express his deepest agonies and his noblest desires through tears. When mingled with prayer, trust, or a deep compassion, tears become a most beautiful and ennobling expression of the believer's faith.

I have no doubt that Jesus delighted in life's wholesome joys and pleasures, even though Scripture nowhere records His smiles or times of laughter. Yet He was so in touch with the heartbreaks of sin all around Him that He wept unashamedly at a tomb, shed tears over the unbelief of Jerusalem, and entered fully into the sorrows of sin-laden humanity.

Our Savior's tears encourage us to be true to our emotions, letting the Holy Spirit use them to overcome barriers and heal relationships. Moistened eyes often convey faith, honesty, caring, and love. Why cry? Because hurting, hardened, unbelieving people need Jesus. And they just might meet Him through our tears.

—Dennis De Haan

Good Grief

Brothers, we do not want you to be ignorant about those who fall asleep, or to grieve like the rest of men, who have no hope. We believe that Jesus died and rose again and so we believe that God will bring with Jesus those who have fallen asleep in him.

According to the Lord's own word, we tell you that we who are still alive, who are left till the coming of the Lord, will certainly not precede those who have fallen asleep. For the Lord himself will come down from heaven, with a loud command, with the voice of the archangel and with the trumpet call of God, and the dead in Christ will rise first. After that, we who are still alive and are left will be caught up together with them in the clouds to meet the Lord in the air. And so we will be with the Lord forever.

Therefore encourage each other with these words.

—1 THESSALONIANS 4:13–18

We often hear the expression "good grief," and perhaps we've wondered, "Is there such a thing as good grief?" The answer is yes. Grief is a healthy and normal response to the death of a loved one or to some other terrible disappointment or loss.

Abraham's experience is an example of good grief. When Sarah died, he mourned for the one he loved. Then, in an act of faith in God's promise, he purchased a burial site in Hebron instead of taking Sarah's body back to his ancestral home. Finally, after placing it in the sepulcher, he went back to his responsibilities (see Genesis 23).

Since grief is natural and healthy, we don't need to feel guilty about it. Well-meaning people may say, "Don't feel bad. Your loved one is better off in heaven." Or, "Try to look on the bright side. Your situation isn't nearly as bad as that of many others." This may all be true, but still we feel very keenly our loss. And we must grieve. As a child of God, however, we can keep our grieving under control by telling the Lord how we feel, asking for His help, focusing on the needs of the living, and picking up our responsibilities. Painful memories will still come from time to time, and we may feel like withdrawing from life's demands. But at such times we should remember that God has left us here for a purpose: to worship Him, to serve Him, and to help others.

With God's help, our grief can become "good grief."

—HERB VANDER LUGT

19

Guilt and Grief

The king [David] asked the Cushite, "Is the young man Absalom safe?" The Cushite replied, "May the enemies of my lord the king and all who rise up to harm you be like that young man."

The king was shaken. He went up to the room over the gateway and wept. As he went, he said: "O my son Absalom! My son, my son Absalom! If only I had died instead of you—O Absalom, my son, my son!"

Joab was told, "The king is weeping and mourning for Absalom." And for the whole army the victory that day was turned into mourning, because on that day the troops heard it said, "The king is grieving for his son." The men stole into the city that day as men steal in who are ashamed when they flee from battle.

The king covered his face and cried aloud, "O my son Absalom! O Absalom, my son, my son!" —2 SAMUEL 18:33–19:8

---

*G*uilt intensifies grief. When you read about David's overwhelming sorrow at the news of his son Absalom's death, you might ask, "Why was it so intense and deep? Did he feel some responsibility for his son's death?"

David had set a bad example for his children by taking many wives. His sin with Bathsheba weakened his example even more. When his son Amnon sexually defiled his sister, Tamar, David was furious but did nothing about it. That incident set the stage for Absalom's murder of Amnon. Even then, David was indecisive in dealing with Absalom; he waited five years before meeting with him. All these failures must have intensified David's grief when Absalom died.

How different is the sorrow of those who do not have deep regrets to add to their pain. For example, a mother went through a terribly difficult time coping with the death of her little boy who was killed in a school bus accident, but she had no remorse. She had been a good mother, and her memory didn't wring from her heart the anguished cry, "If only I . . ."

Lord, show me how to right any wrongs I'm responsible for in my family. Then help me to live so that my grief will be free from guilt when I lose someone who is dear to me.

—HERB VANDER LUGT

Love and Sorrow

When Mary reached the place where Jesus was and saw him, she fell at his feet and said, "Lord, if you had been here, my brother would not have died."

When Jesus saw her weeping, and the Jews who had come along with her also weeping, he was deeply moved in spirit and troubled. . . .

Jesus wept. —JOHN 11:32–33, 35

The tear-stained face of Jesus reveals His true humanity. He wept not just for Lazarus, for He would shortly perform a miracle and raise him from the dead. But when He saw how deeply his friends were grieving, His heart was filled with sympathy, and He identified with them in their loss. We know from the narrative that He loved Mary and Martha and Lazarus, so it's not surprising that He entered into the heartache of those who were so dear to Him. This aspect of our Lord's life shows us that tears that flow from a heart of love are natural.

A woman whose husband had died thought it was wrong to grieve so deeply. Although she knew that her loved one was with the Lord, she could hardly talk about him without weeping. Then one day her pastor pointed out something that was very helpful to her. "When you love deeply," he said, "you make yourself vulnerable. That's why, when a dear one is taken, the suffering is so severe. But not to love is even worse. You cannot fully live without loving!"

Have you lost a loved one? Don't be ashamed of your tears. Deep sadness reveals that you have loved deeply. Grief displeases God when it is self-pity, and when we mourn as one who has no hope. But love and sorrow cannot be separated.

—Henry Bosch

Facing Tomorrow

But if it is preached that Christ has been raised from the dead,
how can some of you say that there is no resurrection of the dead?
If there is no resurrection of the dead, then not even Christ has
been raised. And if Christ has not been raised, our preaching is
useless and so is your faith. . . . And if Christ has not been raised,
your faith is futile; you are still in your sins. Then those also who
have fallen asleep in Christ are lost. If only for this life we have
hope in Christ, we are to be pitied more than all men.

But Christ has indeed been raised from the dead, the first-
fruits of those who have fallen asleep. . . . The last enemy to be
destroyed is death.   —1 CORINTHIANS 15:12–14, 17–20, 26

*D*oreen's life had been enriched by Peter's preaching, but she was more than just a member of his church. Doreen was Peter's wife, and she loved him. So when he died, she felt the loss keenly.

For many weeks, Doreen found it too painful to go to church regularly. And when she did, she couldn't sing.

Several months later, a friend she was visiting in California invited Doreen to a church service. Reluctantly she went. As the congregation sang, "Because He lives, I can face tomorrow," God spoke to her heart and she found herself joining in. In the weeks that followed, sorrow didn't vanish completely, but Doreen could sing again. She could face tomorrow.

When death takes a loved one, grieving is a painful and sometimes prolonged process. At times it may seem impossible to face the simplest tasks, to get through one day. The desire to withdraw is strong.

We can't predict how we would react if a loved one were taken. But the more we nurture our relationship with Christ now, and the more we "let go" of our loved ones before they are taken (by loving them unselfishly), the better able we will be to draw on the comfort and hope found in today's Scripture. And that will help us to face tomorrow.   —DENNIS DE HAAN

Heartaches

As he approached Jerusalem and saw the city, he wept over it and said, "If you, even you, had only known on this day what would bring you peace—but now it is hidden from your eyes. The days will come upon you when your enemies will build an embankment against you and encircle you and hem you in on every side. They will dash you to the ground, you and the children within your walls. They will not leave one stone on another, because you did not recognize the time of God's coming to you."

Then he entered the temple area and began driving out those who were selling. "It is written," he said to them, " 'My house will be a house of prayer'; but you have made it 'a den of robbers.'"

Every day he was teaching at the temple.

–LUKE 19:41–47

*H*eartaches—the world is full of them! A boy is mocked at school because he has an underdeveloped arm. A widow painfully remembers the day her husband committed suicide. Parents grieve over a rebellious son. A man tenderly cares for his wife, who has Alzheimer's disease and doesn't even know him. A minister resigns because of vicious lies told about him. A wife anguishes over her husband's unfaithfulness.

Such heartaches have caused some people to drop out of life. Other hurting folks have gone to the opposite extreme, trying to lose themselves in a flurry of activity.

We can learn how to handle our heartaches by looking at the life of Jesus. His heart was breaking as He contemplated what would happen to Jerusalem. He let Himself cry (Luke 19:41). Then He continued the work He came to do—confronting sin, teaching the people, and instructing His disciples.

If your heart is aching, admit your hurt to yourself, to others, and to God. This will open the door to receiving the help you need from the Lord and from people who care. Then choose to get involved in life by worshiping, loving, caring, and working. As you do, your deep hurt will lessen and your joy will increase.   —HERB VANDER LUGT

Grandpa's Last Hymn

When evening came, Jesus was reclining at the table with the Twelve. . . .

While they were eating, Jesus took bread, gave thanks and broke it, and gave it to his disciples, saying, "Take and eat; this is my body." Then he took the cup, gave thanks and offered it to them, saying, "Drink from it, all of you. This is my blood of the covenant, which is poured out for many for the forgiveness of sins. I tell you, I will not drink of this fruit of the vine from now on until that day when I drink it anew with you in my Father's kingdom."

When they had sung a hymn, they went out to the Mount of Olives. —MATTHEW 26:20, 26–30

As our Lord faced the awful prospect of dying on the cross, He concluded the first communion service with the singing of a hymn. By this He showed us as believers that we can meet the "last enemy" with confidence and joy when we have faith in God and His sustaining grace.

Grandpa Bosch was a dear saint who experienced this peace as he came to the end of his life. I remember hearing my parents tell of his final moments. Shortly after the turn of the century, grandfather became afflicted with a serious heart ailment. In spite of all efforts by the doctor to relieve his condition, he steadily grew worse. After three trying days and nights, he realized that death was near. Calling his children to his side, he spoke to each of them lovingly. Then he said, "Let's part with a hymn." His weak voice quavered as he sang, "My hope is built on nothing less than Jesus' blood and righteousness." But it seemed a bit stronger when he came to his favorite third stanza, "His oath, His covenant, His blood support me in the whelming flood; when all around my soul gives way, He then is all my hope and stay." With tear-filled eyes the others joined in on the chorus, "On Christ, the solid rock, I stand—all other ground is sinking sand. All other ground is sinking sand." After a tender word of spiritual admonition, Grandpa closed his eyes and went to be with the Lord.

If we live for God daily and rely upon Him, then in the face of death we too will have the peace Grandpa had when he sang that parting hymn.   —HENRY BOSCH

Withering Grass—
Wilting Flowers

A voice says, "Cry out."
   And I said, "What shall I cry?"

"All men are like grass,
   and all their glory is like the flowers of the field.
The grass withers and the flowers fall,
   because the breath of the LORD blows on them.
   Surely the people are grass.
The grass withers and the flowers fall,
   but the word of our God stands forever."

—ISAIAH 40:6–8

A heavy dew often forms during the night in Palestine, and the early riser will see the green fields and colorful flowers sparkling with the beauty of those droplets under the first rays of the sun. But in a short time the dew vanishes, the grass withers, and the flowers fade. The prophet likens the swiftness with which this loveliness disappears to our earthly existence.

I was reminded of those words when one of my brothers died suddenly after suffering a heart attack. My wife and I received the news about 2:00 a.m. and hurried to the hospital. Through our tears we viewed his lifeless body. We could hardly believe our eyes. He was only forty-eight, had enjoyed good health, and had been extremely active as a professor, scientist, and church worker. It seemed a tragedy that he had to leave his dearly loved wife and family, and that hundreds of college students would be deprived of a trusted friend and wise counselor. Yes, death often comes unbidden, for "all flesh is grass" (Isaiah 40:6).

Thank the Lord, this isn't the whole story, for we also read, "But the word of our God stands forever" (v. 8). God's promises are eternally true, and since the Bible is literally filled with assurances that all who believe on Jesus receive everlasting life, we have the comfort that my brother is with Christ, resting from all his labors and waiting for the glorious day of resurrection and reunion.

Our bodies are indeed like withering grass and wilting flowers, but we can rejoice in the knowledge that eternal glory awaits all who place their trust in the Lord.

—HERB VANDER LUGT

Confidence and Hope

I declare to you, brothers, that flesh and blood cannot inherit the kingdom of God, nor does the perishable inherit the imperishable. Listen, I tell you a mystery: We will not all sleep, but we will all be changed—in a flash, in the twinkling of an eye, at the last trumpet. For the trumpet will sound, the dead will be raised imperishable, and we will be changed. For the perishable must clothe itself with the imperishable, and the mortal with immortality. When the perishable has been clothed with the imperishable, and the mortal with immortality, then the saying that is written will come true: "Death has been swallowed up in victory."

> *"Where, O death, is your victory?*
> *Where, O death, is your sting?"*
>
> —1 CORINTHIANS 15:50–55

$\mathcal{A}$ group of medical students in a Toronto hospital chose to work with dying patients as part of their course of study. When the staff psychologist inquired about their reason for doing this, he received some interesting replies. They all acknowledged having fears about death and thought that exposure to those who were about to leave this life would somehow help them overcome their anxiety. Like most human beings, these young men dreaded the reality of someday having to face eternity.

By contrast, the Christian's attitude toward death can be filled with confidence and hope. During his last illness, the great reformer John Knox called his wife to his bedside and asked her to read 1 Corinthians 15. When she finished that wonderful passage on the believer's resurrection, he turned to her and said, "Ah, is that not a comforting chapter?" While death is described in the Bible as an enemy, the Lord Jesus has robbed it of its sting (1 Corinthians 15:55).

"The grave is lighted with Immanuel's love," wrote J. R. Macduff. "Although the most ominous of all life's clouds, it forms the background for God's brightest rainbow! Earth will not hold our physical bodies forever. . . . A glorious springtime of new life is promised when the mortal shall put on immortality and the corruptible shall be clothed with incorruption."

Since the Savior has vanquished death, its power holds no terror for the Christian. We know the "valley of the shadow" will only give way to the glorious light of eternal life. What true comfort this brings! —PAUL VAN GORDER

Moses and the Undertaker

Then Moses climbed Mount Nebo from the plains of Moab to the top of Pisgah, across from Jericho. There the LORD showed him the whole land—from Gilead to Dan, all of Naphtali, the territory of Ephraim and Manasseh, all the land of Judah as far as the western sea, the Negev and the whole region from the Valley of Jericho, the City of Palms, as far as Zoar. Then the LORD said to him, "This is the land I promised on oath to Abraham, Isaac and Jacob when I said, 'I will give it to your descendants.' I have let you see it with your eyes, but you will not cross over into it."

And Moses the servant of the LORD died there in Moab, as the LORD had said. He buried him in Moab, in the valley opposite Beth Peor, but to this day no one knows where his grave is. . . . The Israelites grieved for Moses in the plains of Moab thirty days, until the time of weeping and mourning was over.

—DEUTERONOMY 34:1–6, 8

All of us must eventually die unless Jesus comes first! Some go like Moses at the zenith of their greatness, some when on the threshold of their careers, but all depart when and where the heavenly Father chooses. There are no accidents with Him. How glorious to be prepared by grace for this momentous event and like Moses to be "laid to rest" by God Himself!

Ivor Powell, in his book *Bible Cameos*, gives this imaginative picture of how the Lord took Moses:

> Very slowly Moses climbed the hill, to be the central figure in the most solemn event of his career. Perhaps he paused at the turn of the road to look back at his beloved followers, and then resolutely he climbed to keep his appointment with God. . . . Then the Lord lifted His dear friend, and in the everlasting arms Moses was carried to the prepared grave. Relatives and friends were conspicuously absent; only the Undertaker was present. It seems a wonderful thing that He who created the world should reserve for Himself the honor of performing the last act over that still body. . . . Yes, God buried him in some quiet corner where the flowers could bow in graceful salute and where the birds could sing over his grave.

In a spiritual sense, that is true for all who die in the Lord. The grieving who are left behind, have this comfort: God has received their loved one unto Himself.　　—HENRY BOSCH

A Unity that Survives Death

Then the Sadducees, who say there is no resurrection, came to him with a question. "Teacher," they said, "Moses wrote for us that if a man's brother dies and leaves a wife but no children, the man must marry the widow and have children for his brother. Now there were seven brothers. The first one married and died without leaving any children. The second one married the widow, but he also died, leaving no child. It was the same with the third. In fact, none of the seven left any children. Last of all, the woman died too. At the resurrection whose wife will she be, since the seven were married to her?"

Jesus replied, "Are you not in error because you do not know the Scriptures or the power of God? When the dead rise, they will neither marry nor be given in marriage; they will be like the angels in heaven. Now about the dead rising—have you not read in the book of Moses, in the account of the bush, how God said to him, 'I am the God of Abraham, the God of Isaac, and the God of Jacob'? He is not the God of the dead, but of the living. You are badly mistaken!"   —MARK 12:18-27

In our Scripture reading, the Lord Jesus denounced the Sadducees, who said there was no resurrection and contended that man had no identity after death. He reminded them that Jehovah speaks of Himself in the present tense as the God of Abraham, Isaac, and Jacob, and that this implied their conscious existence in the realms of the blest. In Romans 14:8, we are told that whether we live or die we are still in God's keeping. As believers we should not therefore linger too long at the graveside of those who have gone to be with the Lord; for they are now dwelling in the blessed presence of God, untouched by sin or sorrow.

Perhaps you have heard the old poem about a man who met a little girl and asked her how many people were in her family. "There are seven of us," she replied; "two brothers gone to sea, one is living in a faraway country, two of us lying in the churchyard, and mother and I who live at home." The man quickly pointed out that if two of the seven were dead, there were actually only five left. Mentioning each of their names, the girl insisted, "But, good sir, we still are seven!" She was entirely correct as a Christian in counting those who had joined the heavenly choir, for the apostle Paul speaks in Ephesians 3:15 of "the whole family in heaven and on earth" as still being one in the Lord.

With a singing heart of faith, let us remember that we have a continuing unity with all believers that transcends death. We can therefore be sure of meeting our loved ones again when we see Christ.
—HENRY BOSCH

"Alive! Alive"

Bethany was less than two miles from Jerusalem, and many Jews had come to Martha and Mary to comfort them in the loss of their brother. When Martha heard that Jesus was coming, she went out to meet him, but Mary stayed at home.

"Lord," Martha said to Jesus, "if you had been here, my brother would not have died. But I know that even now God will give you whatever you ask."

Jesus said to her, "Your brother will rise again."

Martha answered, "I know he will rise again in the resurrection at the last day."

Jesus said to her, "I am the resurrection and the life. He who believes in me will live, even though he dies; and whoever lives and believes in me will never die. Do you believe this?"

—JOHN 11:17–26

Brothers, we do not want you to be ignorant about those who fall asleep, or to grieve like the rest of men, who have no hope. We believe that Jesus died and rose again and so we believe that God will bring with Jesus those who have fallen asleep in him.

—1 THESSALONIANS 4:13–14

---

*T*he death of eleven-year-old Willie Lincoln on February 20,1862, came as a devastating blow to the President. At times he covered his face with his hands and wept convulsively. In the days that followed, his spirits were so low that he could hardly resume his work. The first Thursday after his son died, Mr. Lincoln shut himself in his room, and no one knew to what extent he gave way to his sorrow. The next week it was the same.

Then Lincoln received a visit from Dr. Francis Vinton of Trinity Church in New York, who told him he was behaving like a heathen and that it was a sin to give way so completely to his grief. "Your son is alive in Paradise," he said. At first Lincoln seemed deaf to his words—then somehow they reached him. "Alive? Surely you mock me!" "No, sir," said Dr. Vinton. "It is a most comforting doctrine of the church, founded upon the words of Christ Himself." For a few minutes the President sobbed and repeated, "Alive! Alive!" After that he no longer shut himself up, and with a mighty effort he turned his attention to the affairs of state.

Losing a loved one can bring on deep depression, and Christians are not immune to the paralyzing effect of this emotional trauma. The pain of bereavement can be severe, and the shedding of tears helps in healing the "wound." Yet, we must resist the tendency to "stop living" because of our grief. True, we sorrow, but not "as others who have no hope." Difficult as it is, we must take up life again, confident that our saved loved one is alive—alive in the presence of Jesus.   —DENNIS DE HAAN

Joy in Sorrow

Yet I am always with you;
*   you hold me by my right hand.*
You guide me with your counsel,
*   and afterward you will take me into glory.*
Whom have I in heaven but you?
*   And earth has nothing I desire besides you.*
My flesh and my heart may fail,
*   but God is the strength of my heart*
*   and my portion forever.*

—PSALM 73:23–26

Children of God need not fear death. We may have a feeling of dread as we think about the discomforts that sometimes accompany dying. But after we say farewell to this world, we will be carried by the angels to the gates of paradise. There all is light, joy, peace, and pleasures forevermore.

On the last day of her life, the gifted hymn writer Frances Havergal asked a friend to read Isaiah 42. When she finished the verse, "I, the LORD, have called you in righteousness, and will hold your hand; I will keep you," Miss Havergal stopped her (v. 6). "Called, held, kept," she whispered. "That's enough. I'll just go home to Glory on those words!" A few minutes later her soul entered heaven.

When the Lord saves us out of darkness and brings us into His marvelous light, He leads and keeps us until we are safe in His everlasting mansions.

The early Christians, even though their hearts were torn by bereavement, often celebrated a believer's death rather than mourning it. In the old burying places in Rome called catacombs, the epitaphs speak of joy and victory. One of these inscriptions reads: "Tentianus vivit"—that is, "Tentianus lives." The first-century believers knew that the spirit lives on and that the body will eventually be resurrected.

The Christian view of death gives us joy in sorrow and enables us to say with David, "Yea, though I walk through the valley of the shadow of death, I will fear no evil."

—HENRY BOSCH

"It's Bedtime!"

I have set the LORD always before me.
  Because he is at my right hand,
  I will not be shaken.
Therefore my heart is glad and my tongue rejoices;
  my body also will rest secure,
because you will not abandon me to the grave,
  nor will you let your Holy One see decay.
You have made known to me the path of life;
  you will fill me with joy in your presence,
  with eternal pleasures at your right hand.

—PSALM 16:8–11

In his book *The Best Is Yet To Be*, Henry Durbanville recalled that as a boy, when the shadows of evening lengthened and darkness fell, he would hear his mother call, "Henry, it's bedtime!" Typical of all small boys, he resisted the idea of leaving his friends, putting his toys away, and going to his room for the night. Yet deep within his heart he knew very well that sleep was necessary.

Durbanville made this spiritual application for the Christian who senses the end of life drawing near: "Death is both affectionate and stern. When the right moment comes, she says to us, 'It's your bedtime.' Oh, we may protest a little, but we know very well that the hour for rest has come, and in our hearts we are actually longing for it."

The thought of dying can fill even a Christian's heart with mixed emotions. When we think of leaving our loved ones, it may cause the tears to flow. The breaking of close human ties does hurt. On the other hand, there is the anticipation of resting from our labors and being in the presence of the Lord.

If we have placed our faith in Christ, we can look forward to the joy and release that will be ours when we hear the evening call, "Come Home. It's bedtime!" —RICHARD DE HAAN

My Savior Is There!

Now we know that if the earthly tent we live in is destroyed, we have a building from God, an eternal house in heaven, not built by human hands. Meanwhile we groan, longing to be clothed with our heavenly dwelling, because when we are clothed, we will not be found naked. For while we are in this tent, we groan and are burdened, because we do not wish to be unclothed but to be clothed with our heavenly dwelling, so that what is mortal may be swallowed up by life. Now it is God who has made us for this very purpose and has given us the Spirit as a deposit, guaranteeing what is to come.

Therefore we are always confident and know that as long as we are at home in the body we are away from the Lord. We live by faith, not by sight. We are confident, I say, and would prefer to be away from the body and at home with the Lord. So we make it our goal to please him, whether we are at home in the body or away from it. —2 CORINTHIANS 5:1–9

*D*ying will be a brand-new experience for all of us. Nothing else in life is quite like it. Yet the person who knows Jesus as Savior can face death with confidence. He has the assurance that Christ will always be with him. In fact, leaving this life can be a blessing. The apostle Paul looked upon it as "gain," for he anticipated being ushered into the presence of his Savior and Lord.

In his book *The Best Is Yet To Be*, Henry Durbanville told the story of a man who lay dying and was fearful, even though he was a born-again Christian. He expressed his feelings to his Christian doctor. The physician was silent, not knowing what to say. Just then a whining and scratching was heard at the door. When the doctor opened it, in bounded his big, beautiful dog that often went with him as he made house calls. The dog was glad to see his master. Sensing an opportunity to comfort his troubled patient, the doctor said, "My dog has never been in your room before, and he didn't know what it was like in here. But he knew I was here and that was enough. In the same way, I'm looking forward to heaven. I don't know much about it, but I know my Savior is there. And that's all I need to know!"

Unless Jesus returns first, the day will come when we will have to walk "through the valley of the shadow of death." While it's natural to wonder what it will be like, we don't have to live in fear. When we arrive at death's door, we can have confidence because we know He is on the other side!

—RICHARD DE HAAN

When Death Is Gain

Listen, I tell you a mystery: We will not all sleep, but we will all be changed—in a flash, in the twinkling of an eye, at the last trumpet. For the trumpet will sound, the dead will be raised imperishable, and we will be changed. For the perishable must clothe itself with the imperishable, and the mortal with immortality. When the perishable has been clothed with the imperishable, and the mortal with immortality, then the saying that is written will come true: "Death has been swallowed up in victory."
—1 CORINTHIANS 15:51–54

For to me, to live is Christ and to die is gain.
—PHILIPPIANS 1:21

*M*any phrases have been coined by literary men seeking to soften the harshness of the word *death*. William Shakespeare called it "a necessary end." A more recent poet called it "the cool enfolding finale." And Ingersoll, an agnostic, seeking to find some comfort in the vacuum of his infidelity, called it "the fine serenity of death."

How different are the forthright, stirring words of Scripture! Under inspiration, Paul said, "to die is gain," for it results in our being "present with the Lord." That's why the early Christians looked forward to their home going as a happy entrance into Glory—not a dreaded departure from this earth.

Believers in every age have experienced that same confidence in their final moments on earth. For example, William Anderson of Dallas had been ill with an incurable disease. Although he had rallied and seemed to be a little better, he knew that his time to leave this earth was near. So, calling his mother to come closer to his bed, he whispered, "I want to tell you something. In spite of what the doctors are saying, I'm going to get to heaven before you do." Then, smiling peacefully, he shut his eyes, and within a few minutes his soul had winged its way to Glory. Because Anderson's faith was fixed on Jesus, fear was banished, and he joyfully anticipated going to be with the Lord.

Dear one in Christ, be assured that your final farewell to this world will usher you into eternal bliss. Because the Savior has conquered the grave and forgiven your sin, your death will be gain.

—Henry Bosch

"I Saw an Eagle Die"

But Stephen, full of the Holy Spirit, looked up to heaven and saw the glory of God, and Jesus standing at the right hand of God. "Look," he said, "I see heaven open and the Son of Man standing at the right hand of God."

At this they covered their ears and, yelling at the top of their voices, they all rushed at him, dragged him out of the city and began to stone him. . . .

While they were stoning him, Stephen prayed, "Lord Jesus, receive my spirit." Then he fell on his knees and cried out, "Lord, do not hold this sin against them." When he had said this, he fell asleep.

—ACTS 7:55–60

I was captivated by this brief sentence: "I saw an eagle die." The writer Everett L. Fullam had just pointed out that when an eagle senses it is about to die, it leaves its nest, flies to a rock, fastens its talons on it, looks straight into the setting sun, and dies. I fully expected Fullam to give a first-hand description of an eagle's last hours. Instead, he told how his father, who was a Christian, "saw beyond the sun" just before he died. Unexpectedly awakening from a coma, the dying man spoke appreciatively to each family member at his bedside. Then, noticing the tears coursing down their cheeks, he told them that if they could hear what he had been hearing and see what he had just seen, they would not want him to recover. Finally, gathering up his last ounce of strength, he exclaimed, "Rejoice with me! This is my crowning day." With that he died.

I believe Everett Fullam's father may have had a preview of heaven. The biblical basis for this idea is the death of Stephen. Just before he left this life, he looked into heaven and saw Jesus. Most believers don't have an experience like that. But with the eye of faith all believers can be sure of the glories of the invisible world that awaits them.

Hebrews 11:1 tells us that faith gives substance to our hopes and makes us certain of realities that cannot be seen with the physical eye. Therefore, we can have the assurance that when we face death, we can do so with serenity and hope. Then those who see us in that hour will be able to say, "I saw an eagle die."

—HERB VANDER LUGT

An Enemy and a Friend

But Christ has indeed been raised from the dead, the firstfruits of those who have fallen asleep. For since death came through a man, the resurrection of the dead comes also through a man. For as in Adam all die, so in Christ all will be made alive. But each in his own turn: Christ, the firstfruits; then, when he comes, those who belong to him. Then the end will come, when he hands over the kingdom to God the Father after he has destroyed all dominion, authority and power. For he must reign until he has put all his enemies under his feet.

The last enemy to be destroyed is death.

—1 CORINTHIANS 15:12–28

Most non-Christians respond to death with morbid pessimism or unrealistic optimism. Some lose all control of their emotions and are inconsolable. Others say things they don't really believe, such as, "Dad is now playing chess with Uncle George." Even some ministers are guilty of offering only sentimental poetry and eloquent nothings in their funeral sermons.

By contrast, Christians neither glamorize death as some Eastern mystics do, nor dread it as naturalistic humanists do. Instead, they see it for what it is—both an enemy and a friend. Because it is the result of sin, death causes great distress. But it is also a friend in disguise—the means by which a believer in Christ is translated from the pain of earth to the pleasures of heaven.

Christian realism about death is beautifully expressed in a poem George McDonald wrote to his sorrowing wife when their daughter died. He began by telling her that she wouldn't find consolation in lovely but empty sentiments that he called "pleasant fancies of a half-held creed." He then pointed out that the Great Shepherd had gone before and prepared the way for their daughter. McDonald reminded her that they were both moving along day by day toward that same destination. In closing, he said, "We seek not death, but still we climb the stairs where death is one wide landing to the rooms above."

The Christian need not fear death, for we know that Jesus broke its power through His own death and glorious resurrection. Yes, it is an enemy, but it is also a friend.

—HERB VANDER LUGT

Ready to Go

I will exalt you, O Lord,
> for you lifted me out of the depths
> and did not let my enemies gloat over me.
O Lord my God, I called to you for help
> and you healed me.
O Lord, you brought me up from the grave;
> you spared me from going down into the pit.

Sing to the Lord, you saints of his;
> praise his holy name.
For his anger lasts only a moment,
> but his favor lasts a lifetime;
weeping may remain for a night,
> but rejoicing comes in the morning.

—PSALM 30:1–5

*L*ife in heaven is far better than anything earth can offer; yet we do our best to avoid dying. If we get sick, we pray for recovery. The psalmist was no different. He began Psalm 30 by praising God for saving him from death (vv. 1-4). Then, he declared that his distress, which reflected God's anger, was only temporary and that God's favor would be everlasting (v. 5). He also told why he became ill and what he learned through his affliction. He had become proud, so God allowed the illness to humble him and to give him a new perspective on life. He saw more clearly than ever that eternal blessedness far outweighs present distress. Closing his song, he rejoiced in the prospect of praising God throughout eternity. God had prepared him so that he could die in peace.

When my mother was in her early sixties, the doctor told her she would soon die from heart failure. She was despondent. She loved life and didn't want to leave her family. We prayed for her recovery, and God graciously answered by giving her twelve more years. Shortly before she died, I asked her, "Mom, do you still dread dying?" With a smile she replied, "No, I'm ready."

Christian, don't feel guilty about not wanting to die. God made you that way. And don't worry about dying. The Lord will prepare you for that day. Keep walking with Him, doing His will, and trusting Him to meet your need. When you are called Home, God will give grace and you'll be ready to go.

—HERB VANDER LUGT

God's Reason

There is a time for everything,
and a season for every activity under heaven:

a time to be born and a time to die . . .

—ECCLESIASTES 3:1–2

I eagerly expect and hope that I will in no way be ashamed, but will have sufficient courage so that now as always Christ will be exalted in my body, whether by life or by death. For to me, to live is Christ and to die is gain. —PHILIPPIANS 1:20–21

In 1983, Paul "Bear" Bryant died unexpectedly, just days after he retired. He was the college football coach with the best win-loss record of all time. Announcing his death, a news reporter quoted Bryant as saying a year earlier, "When I stop coaching football, I'll die." The reporter added, "Presumably that is what happened."

I'm not saying Bryant died for lack of purpose in life, but his words remind us of an important fact: Christians die when God in wisdom decides to take them home. The means may be disease, accident, or old age. But behind what's written on the death certificate is God's reason, and the Bible gives at least three causes.

First, God calls us home when our purpose for being on earth has been fulfilled. Paul said, "I have finished the race" (2 Timothy 4:7). Second, death may spare us suffering. Abijah, the young son of wicked King Jeroboam, became sick and died because in him was found "something good toward the LORD God." His death spared him the terrible judgment that later fell on his father's house (1 Kings 14:1–14). Third, God may chasten through death. Because some Corinthian believers had gotten drunk at their love feasts, God judged them and many died (1 Corinthians 11:21, 30). This seems harsh, but judgment kept them from being "condemned with the world" (v. 32).

When a Christian dies, regardless of circumstance or age, we take comfort in knowing that it is better for that one to be with the Lord than to remain on earth. —DENNIS DE HAAN

When Life Begins

Even though I walk
  through the valley of the shadow of death,
I will fear no evil,
  for you are with me;
your rod and your staff,
  they comfort me.

You prepare a table before me
  in the presence of my enemies.
You anoint my head with oil;
  my cup overflows.
Surely goodness and love will follow me
  all the days of my life,
and I will dwell in the house of the LORD
  forever.   —PSALM 23:4–6

In AD 125, a man named Aristides sent a letter to an acquaintance in which he gave this explanation for the rapid spread of Christianity: "If any righteous man among the Christians passes from this world, they rejoice and offer thanks to God, and they escort his body with songs and thanksgiving as if he were setting out from one place to another nearby."

Yes, believers in the Lord Jesus can face death differently from those who don't know Him because they have a hope beyond the grave. There's an old saying that goes, "Life begins at 40." For God's children, however, life—new and glorious living—begins at death when the soul leaves the body and enters into the presence of the Lord. That's why they can face death with such confidence and joy.

Christians' attitudes toward the grave can even be detected in their obituaries. Instead of the usual wording that a loved one has "died" or "passed away," the death notices of believers often express the comforting assurance that they were "called home to be with Jesus," or "went to be with the Lord."

What a remarkable difference there is in the ways an unbeliever and a believer look at death! For one, it's often viewed as a hopeless ending. For the other, it's seen as a joyous beginning.

—RICHARD DE HAAN

"Not Today"

In the course of my life he broke my strength;
*   he cut short my days.*
So I said:
*   "Do not take me away, O my God,*
*   in the midst of my days;*
*   your years go on through all generations.*
                                    —PSALM 102:23–24

The psalmist who wrote today's text desired to hold firmly to life. Even older Christians who long to meet God and be released from earth's sufferings may experience mixed feelings of anticipation and apprehension about dying. This is normal and should not cause needless guilt.

D. J. De Pree was a devoted servant of God. Yet when he neared the end of his ninety-nine-year earthly pilgrimage, he manifested a strong desire to live and an uneasiness about dying. On one occasion, after sitting for a long while, the nurses came into his hospital room to help him back into bed. But D. J. stubbornly refused to leave his chair. "Why won't you get back into bed?" asked his son Max. "Because if I get back into that bed, I will die there," said D. J. "But Dad," said Max, "you've been telling me for weeks you are ready to die." "I am," said his father, "but not today!"

It's natural to cling to life and to feel some reticence about moving into the unknown—even for a Christian. So let's be realistic about death. Our love for life is God-given. Death is an enemy and its sting is caused by sin. But Jesus has won for us victory over the grave by His own death and resurrection. So when facing death, our confidence can be real, even though we may say, "Not today." —DENNIS DE HAAN

Comfort in Sorrow

And we know that in all things God works for the good of those who love him, who have been called according to his purpose. . . . What, then, shall we say in response to this? If God is for us, who can be against us? He who did not spare his own Son, but gave him up for us all—how will he not also, along with him, graciously give us all things? . . .

Who shall separate us from the love of Christ? Shall trouble or hardship or persecution or famine or nakedness or danger or sword? As it is written:

"For your sake we face death all day long;
we are considered as sheep to be slaughtered."

No, in all these things we are more than conquerors through him who loved us. For I am convinced that neither death nor life, neither angels nor demons, neither the present nor the future, nor any powers, neither height nor depth, nor anything else in all creation, will be able to separate us from the love of God that is in Christ Jesus our Lord.

—ROMANS 8:28, 31–32, 35–39

*D*eath is life's final tragedy. The great equalizer. An ever-looming reminder of mortality. The ultimate thief.

If you've lost a loved one, you understand death's awful finality. You may have groped through the void, searching for answers. You may have relived the haunting emptiness of that final goodbye.

Death took my sister in 1987. It robbed her two sons of their mother to guide them through high school. It stole my parents' only daughter. Without Alice, the world became a less friendly, less gentle, less understanding place. The thought of her parting has always been, and will always be, painful. Yet I have learned about God's love through this loss. I've come to realize that not even the grief we experience at the death of a loved one can "separate us from the love of God." I have found great comfort in these truths:

- Whatever God does, even if it is not what we want Him to do, is right (Genesis 18:25).
- What God has prepared for us is far better than what we leave behind (John 14:1-6).
- God's grace is sufficient for all of life's heartaches (2 Corinthians 2:9).

None of us finds it easy to say goodbye to a loved one at death. Yet God comforts we who are left behind, as we trust in Christ.

—DAVE BRANON

A Family Matter

Then Jacob called for his sons and said: "Gather around so I can tell you what will happen to you in days to come. . . .

Then he gave them these instructions: "I am about to be gathered to my people. Bury me with my fathers in the cave in the field of Ephron the Hittite, the cave in the field of Machpelah, near Mamre in Canaan, which Abraham bought as a burial place from Ephron the Hittite, along with the field. There Abraham and his wife Sarah were buried, there Isaac and his wife Rebekah were buried, and there I buried Leah. The field and the cave in it were bought from the Hittites"

When Jacob had finished giving instructions to his sons, he drew his feet up into the bed, breathed his last and was gathered to his people.   —GENESIS 49:1, 29–33

woman was very upset to see a bereaved husband allow his young children to view the body of their mother in the casket. She said, "We should do all we can to shield children from the fact of death."

That woman may have meant well, but God has designed children so they can handle death, even of a parent or sibling. Most do not feel sorrow as keenly as they will when they get older. And they are usually open to believe us when we tell them that Christians go to live with Jesus when they die. I've observed a remarkable degree of understanding and strength in children when a loved one has died.

When Jacob knew he was about to die, he summoned his sons and spoke to them frankly (Genesis 49). He conferred a blessing on them and on his two grandsons. He didn't know as much about the hereafter as we do today since Jesus rose from the grave. But his trust in God and the calm confidence with which he faced death undoubtedly left a lasting impression on all who were gathered at his bedside.

Let's not be afraid to talk about death with our family. We should discuss it openly and honestly—even with young children. It is not a subject that Christians should avoid, but it's a family matter to be faced with realism and the hope we have in Christ. —HERB VANDER LUGT

Heading Home

It was now about the sixth hour, and darkness came over the whole land until the ninth hour, for the sun stopped shining. And the curtain of the temple was torn in two. Jesus called out with a loud voice, "Father, into your hands I commit my spirit." When he had said this, he breathed his last. . . .

On the first day of the week, very early in the morning, the women took the spices they had prepared and went to the tomb. They found the stone rolled away from the tomb, but when they entered, they did not find the body of the Lord Jesus. While they were wondering about this, suddenly two men in clothes that gleamed like lightning stood beside them. In their fright the women bowed down with their faces to the ground, but the men said to them, "Why do you look for the living among the dead? He is not here; he has risen!   —LUKE 23:44–46; 24:1–6

---

*Y*ears ago a headline in our local newspaper read, "One of Five Heading Home!" The article reported that my brother Pete, one of five of us in the service during World War II, was coming home on leave after three years of fighting in the South Pacific. My parents and younger brothers who were still at home were excited. But their joy suddenly turned to grief when a telegram came announcing the death of my brother Cornelius. One of the younger boys said, "That headline was true twice. 'Heading home' describes Cornie as well as Pete."

Our Lord's final statement from the cross was the calm declaration, "Father, into your hands I commit my spirit." Having said this, He let His spirit leave His body and return to the place of glory He had left thirty-three years earlier. Then on Easter morning He received His new body, in which He now lives as the glorified God-man. He is home, where He welcomes all believers when they die.

Death is a home going for all who have received Jesus. We go to be with our heavenly Father, with our Savior, with believers of all the ages, and with our loved ones who've gone ahead of us. Heading home—what a blessed description of a Christian's death!　　　　　　　　　　　　　—HERB VANDER LUGT

The Cape of Good Hope

But we see Jesus, who was made a little lower than the angels, now crowned with glory and honor because he suffered death, so that by the grace of God he might taste death for everyone. In bringing many sons to glory, it was fitting that God, for whom and through whom everything exists, should make the author of their salvation perfect through suffering. Both the one who makes men holy and those who are made holy are of the same family. So Jesus is not ashamed to call them brothers. . . .

Since the children have flesh and blood, he too shared in their humanity so that by his death he might destroy him who holds the power of death—that is, the devil—and free those who all their lives were held in slavery by their fear of death.

—HEBREWS 2:9–11, 14

At the southern tip of Africa, a cape jutting out into the ocean once caused sailors great anxiety. Many who attempted to sail around it were lost in the swirling seas. Because adverse weather conditions so often prevailed there, the region was named the Cape of Storms. A Portuguese captain determined to find a safe route through those treacherous waters so his countrymen could reach Cathay and the riches of the East Indies in safety. He succeeded, and the area was renamed the Cape of Good Hope.

We all face a great storm called death. But our Lord has already traveled through it safely and has provided a way for us to do the same. By His crucifixion and resurrection, Christ abolished eternal death for every believer and has permanently established our fellowship with Him in heaven. Although this "last enemy," physical death, can touch us temporarily, its brief control over our earthly body will end at the resurrection. The sting of death has been removed!

Now all who know Christ as Savior can face life's final voyage with confidence. Even though the sea may be rough, we will experience no terror as we pass through the "cape of good hope" and into heaven's harbor. The Master Helmsman Himself has assured our safe passage. —HENRY BOSCH

When Someone Is Gone

Brothers, we do not want you to be ignorant about those who fall asleep, or to grieve like the rest of men, who have no hope. We believe that Jesus died and rose again and so we believe that God will bring with Jesus those who have fallen asleep in him. According to the Lord's own word, we tell you that we who are still alive, who are left till the coming of the Lord, will certainly not precede those who have fallen asleep. For the Lord himself will come down from heaven, with a loud command, with the voice of the archangel and with the trumpet call of God, and the dead in Christ will rise first. After that, we who are still alive and are left will be caught up together with them in the clouds to meet the Lord in the air. And so we will be with the Lord forever. Therefore encourage each other with these words.

—1 THESSALONIANS 4:13–18

It was one of those rare times at our house when there was only one child around. Stevie's older sisters were off at camps and on mission trips, so it was a good time for a father-son airport outing.

We had just left McDonald's and were on our way to visit the cockpit of a DC-9 when Stevie surprised me. After I said, "This is fun, isn't it?" he replied, almost sadly, "Yeah, but it's not as much fun without Melissa."

I figured his mind would be filled with thoughts of airplanes and burgers, so for him to think about his eight-year-old sister was unexpected.

His sentiment reminded me of how significant our loved ones are to us. When they're away, our activities can't make us stop thinking of them and wishing they were with us. That truth has special significance if we have loved ones who have died. The loss of their companionship is painful. Life is not the same without them.

In our sadness, though, God comforts us with the promise of 1 Thessalonians 4, which tells us that we do not need to "sorrow as others who have no hope" (v. 13 NKJV). We can look forward to the time when Jesus returns and we will be reunited with our believing loved ones. That truth is a big comfort when someone is gone.

—DAVE BRANON

Faith That Works

"Do not let your hearts be troubled. Trust in God; trust also in me. In my Father's house are many rooms; if it were not so, I would have told you. I am going there to prepare a place for you. And if I go and prepare a place for you, I will come back and take you to be with me that you also may be where I am. You know the way to the place where I am going." —JOHN 14:1–4

I read about a family who lost three children to diphtheria in the same week. Only a three-year-old girl escaped the disease. On the following Easter morning, the father, mother, and child attended church. Because the father was the Sunday school superintendent, he led the session when all the classes met together. As he read the Easter message from the Bible, many were weeping, but the father and mother remained calm and serene.

When Sunday school was over, a fifteen-year-old boy was walking home with his father. "The superintendent and his wife must really believe the Easter story," said the boy. His father answered, "All Christians do." "Not the way they do!" replied the young man.

How we react under trial demonstrates the depth of our convictions. This is not to say that a true Christian will not weep at the loss of a loved one. However, knowing that all believers who die go into Christ's presence, we need not "sorrow as others who have no hope" (1 Thessalonians 4:13 NKJV). We can say, "Thank You, Lord," because we know He can be trusted to do what is best. The prophet said it well: "Though the fig tree may not blossom, nor fruit be on the vines; . . . yet I will rejoice in the LORD" (Habakkuk 3:17-18 NKJV).

—RICHARD DE HAAN

When the End
Is a Beginning

I declare to you, brothers, that flesh and blood cannot inherit the kingdom of God, nor does the perishable inherit the imperishable. Listen, I tell you a mystery: We will not all sleep, but we will all be changed—in a flash, in the twinkling of an eye, at the last trumpet. For the trumpet will sound, the dead will be raised imperishable, and we will be changed. For the perishable must clothe itself with the imperishable, and the mortal with immortality. When the perishable has been clothed with the imperishable, and the mortal with immortality, then the saying that is written will come true: "Death has been swallowed up in victory."

> *"Where, O death, is your victory?*
> *Where, O death, is your sting?"*

—1 CORINTHIANS 15:50–55

*O*ur faith in Jesus Christ ought to make a difference in the way we live—and in the way we die.

God wants us to live with zest and happiness. Indeed, Jesus said He came to offer us abundant life (John 10:10). Paul too affirmed that God "richly provides us with everything for our enjoyment" (1 Timothy 6:17).

Yet we can't escape the fact that our days on earth are numbered. So it is wise to think about our inevitable appointment with death (Hebrews 9:27).

Is our attitude toward our departure from this world like that of famous scientist Marie Curie, who with her husband Pierre discovered radium? When he was accidentally killed, she lamented, "It is the end of everything, everything, everything!"

Our attitude should be radically different. Because of our trust in the death-conquering Savior, we can say as a young German theologian did the night before the Nazis hanged him in 1945, "For me, this is the beginning."

For the believer, death is the end of all pain, loneliness, and sorrow, the end of whatever has made this life less than abundant, and the beginning of unimaginable blessing (Revelation 21:1–6). That prospect enables us to exclaim, "Where, O death, is your sting?" (1 Corinthians 15:55).   —VERNON GROUNDS

The Right Time?

The LORD is gracious and righteous;
    our God is full of compassion. . . .
How can I repay the LORD
    for all his goodness to me?
I will lift up the cup of salvation
    and call on the name of the LORD.
I will fulfill my vows to the LORD
    in the presence of all his people.
Precious in the sight of the LORD
    is the death of his saints.

—PSALM 116:5, 12–15

*I*t was time. Not the time any of us would have chosen. Yet it was God's time. And we had gathered to accept it.

Specifically, the time was the day in God's appointed timetable when my dad would be taken from us in death. His eighty-three good years of service to his Savior and his fifty-one loyal years of family leadership were over. His strong, determined body had at last succumbed to the relentless processes of aging and disease.

Yet it was Christmastime. The time of bright lights, joyous songs, and talk of Jesus' birth. It was time for anticipation, children's excitement, and peace on earth.

It was not a time, it would seem, to think about funeral arrangements and saying goodbye. How could this be the right time?

It was the right time because it was God's time. It was time for Dad to stop suffering. It was time for him to spend Christmas with Jesus. It was time for reunion with my sister in heaven—and how Dad liked reunions!

It was the right time because God never errs. He knew that my father's work was complete, his influence would live on, and his legacy was secure. He knew what He was doing. Dad was home for Christmas. It was time—God's time.

—DAVE BRANON

Life Is a Gift

So in the course of time Hannah conceived and gave birth to a son. She named him Samuel, saying, "Because I asked the LORD for him." . . .

After he was weaned, she took the boy with her, young as he was, along with a three-year-old bull, an ephah of flour and a skin of wine, and brought him to the house of the LORD at Shiloh. When they had slaughtered the bull, they brought the boy to Eli, and she said to him, "As surely as you live, my lord, I am the woman who stood here beside you praying to the LORD. I prayed for this child, and the LORD has granted me what I asked of him. So now I give him to the LORD. For his whole life he will be given over to the LORD." And he worshiped the LORD there.

—I SAMUEL 1:20, 24–28

When I was eight years old, a classmate died. At the funeral service I pictured him "safe in the arms of Jesus." This comforted me and made death less fearsome.

The same year, a five-year-old neighbor boy died, and I became very aware of the grief of his parents. They were crushed and actually seemed angry. It was clear to me that they felt death had robbed them of what rightfully belonged to them.

It's understandable that we go through a time of questioning and even anger when someone we love dies. But we need not stay there. Instead of viewing life as a possession, we need to view it as a gift.

Pastor John Claypool and his wife saw their ten-year-old daughter die from leukemia. He said they found peace when they saw that their daughter's life was "a gift—a pure, simple, sheer gift—to be received and handled with gratitude."

In our Bible reading for today, we learn that it was because Hannah viewed her son's life as a gracious gift that she was able to give him back to God (1 Samuel 1:27-28).

We too would do well to make sure we view life as a gift, not a possession. That attitude will increase our appreciation for life and lessen our anger at death.

— HERB VANDER LUGT

He Cares

Do not be afraid of those who kill the body but cannot kill the soul. Rather, be afraid of the One who can destroy both soul and body in hell. Are not two sparrows sold for a penny? Yet not one of them will fall to the ground apart from the will of your Father. And even the very hairs of your head are all numbered. So don't be afraid; you are worth more than many sparrows.

—Matthew 10:28–31

President George H. W. Bush visited Honduras soon after Hurricane Mitch devastated that nation in 1998. Television interviewer Larry King asked Bush if natural disasters like this one shook his belief in God. The president replied by telling of a seventy-three-year-old man who had lost all he owned. Through his tears, the man told Bush with confidence, "Every possession I had is gone, but . . . I have faith in God."

The news that thousands of people have been buried in mud is disturbing and heartbreaking, to say the least. Does God care?

Jesus said that our heavenly Father observes the fall of even a sparrow (Matthew 10:29), so we can be sure that He is aware of each person who dies in disasters such as this, and He grieves. He values each of us so much that He sent His Son to die on the cross for us (Romans 5:8).

When followers of Christ are victims of such a tragedy, family and friends can find great comfort in the words, "Precious in the sight of the Lord is the death of his saints" (Psalm 116:15). The word precious here means "of great significance" or "of great concern."

So when death and tragedy touches your life, remember that God cares. Have faith in Him.   —HERB VANDER LUGT

Painful Farewells

From Miletus, Paul sent to Ephesus for the elders of the church. When they arrived, he said to them: "You know how I lived the whole time I was with you, from the first day I came into the province of Asia. . . . And now, compelled by the Spirit, I am going to Jerusalem, not knowing what will happen to me there. I only know that in every city the Holy Spirit warns me that prison and hardships are facing me. However, I consider my life worth nothing to me, if only I may finish the race and complete the task the Lord Jesus has given me—the task of testifying to the gospel of God's grace.

"Now I know that none of you among whom I have gone about preaching the kingdom will ever see me again. . . . Now I commit you to God and to the word of his grace, which can build you up and give you an inheritance among all those who are sanctified. . . ."

When he had said this, he knelt down with all of them and prayed. They all wept as they embraced him and kissed him. What grieved them most was his statement that they would never see his face again.

—Acts 20:17–18, 22–25, 32, 36–38

Saying goodbye to someone you love can be awkward and difficult. Down deep you wonder, *Will I ever see this person again?* You almost wish you had never gotten so attached. It hurts so much to let go.

I thought of this as I looked at some pictures a young woman had collected during her high school years. She talked to me about several students from abroad who had become her dear friends. When I asked how she had grown so attached to them, she replied, "I don't know. But it sure was hard to say goodbye!"

Sooner or later, we all will experience the tears of separation. The apostle Paul nurtured and taught the believers in Ephesus for three years. But when he had to leave, "They all wept as they embraced him . . . grieved . . . that they would never see his face again" (Acts 20:37–38).

As Christians, we have good reason to establish close ties, even though they will eventually be broken. Our hope in the resurrection to come assures us that someday we will be reunited in the presence of God.

Farewells can be very painful. But don't let that keep you from building close relationships with others who love the Lord. He makes those friendships worthwhile—both now and in eternity!

—MART DE HAAN

At the Cemetery

Jesus said to her, "I am the resurrection and the life. He who believes in me will live, even though he dies; and whoever lives and believes in me will never die. Do you believe this?"

—JOHN 11:25–26

According to the Lord's own word, we tell you that we who are still alive, who are left till the coming of the Lord, will certainly not precede those who have fallen asleep. For the Lord himself will come down from heaven, with a loud command, with the voice of the archangel and with the trumpet call of God, and the dead in Christ will rise first. —1 THESSALONIANS 4:15–16

When a loved one dies and we go to the cemetery, we may join a long processional. We may sit or stand around the gravesite and listen respectfully while the minister commits the body to the earth and reads Bible verses about the resurrection. Then the casket is lowered into the ground. We may return later to leave some flowers and stand with heads bowed in memory and respect. Our loved one is dead, and we know we can never bring him back.

When Jesus went to the cemetery, it was different. His friend Lazarus had died, and when Jesus got to the tomb, He exercised His power and authority. He commanded: "Take away the stone" (John 11:39). "Lazarus, come forth!" (v. 43 NKJV). "Take off the grave clothes and let him go" (v. 44).

We might wish with all our hearts that we could bring a loved one back, but if we were to give those commands nothing would happen. But Jesus has that ability, for He is "the resurrection and the life" (v. 25). His power was demonstrated when Lazarus came out of the tomb—alive!

One day, Jesus will again be "at the cemetery." And when He gives the command, all the dead who believed in Him will "come forth" (John 5:28-29; 1 Thessalonians 4:16). What a day that will be!

—DAVE EGNER

Keep Talking About Jesus

For what I received I passed on to you as of first importance: that Christ died for our sins according to the Scriptures, that he was buried, that he was raised on the third day according to the Scriptures, and that he appeared to Peter, and then to the Twelve. . . .

But Christ has indeed been raised from the dead, the first-fruits of those who have fallen asleep. For since death came through a man, the resurrection of the dead comes also through a man. For as in Adam all die, so in Christ all will be made alive. —1 CORINTHIANS 15:3–5, 20–22

*P*astor Eloy Pacheco said at a funeral for a believer that Jesus is the only lasting source of comfort. Afterward a woman came up to him and said, "You preachers are all alike. All you talk about is Jesus, Jesus, Jesus!"

"That's true," he replied kindly. "What comfort do you have to offer the grieving family?"

She was speechless for a few moments, and then she said, "You're right. At least you have Jesus."

Sooner or later someone dear to us will die, and we'll want to be comforted. A hug, a kind deed, shared tears, and the presence of a friend may ease sorrow's pain just a bit. But these gestures won't answer our most urgent questions: What's beyond the grave? Where is the person now? Will we be reunited in heaven? How can I have the assurance of eternal life?

For the answers to those questions, we must look to Jesus Christ. He is the One who defeated sin and death by dying on the cross and rising from the grave for us (1 Corinthians 15:1-28, 57). Because He lives, all who put their faith in Him will live forever with Him (John 11:25).

When a believer in Christ dies, we who are left behind can find comfort and confidence in Him. So let's keep talking about Jesus.　　　　　—DENNIS DE HAAN

Life Beyond the Grave

After he had said this, he went on to tell them, "Our friend Lazarus has fallen asleep; but I am going there to wake him up."

His disciples replied, "Lord, if he sleeps, he will get better." Jesus had been speaking of his death, but his disciples thought he meant natural sleep. So then he told them plainly, "Lazarus is dead, and for your sake I am glad I was not there, so that you may believe. But let us go to him." . . .

Jesus said to her, "Your brother will rise again."

Martha answered, "I know he will rise again in the resurrection at the last day."

Jesus said to her, "I am the resurrection and the life. He who believes in me will live, even though he dies; and whoever lives and believes in me will never die. Do you believe this?"

—JOHN 11:11–15, 23–26

My beloved husband Bill died of cancer at the age of forty-eight. One tearful morning I read John 11, the story about Jesus raising Lazarus from the dead. I was reassured by two truths I found in Jesus' words to His disciples on their way to Lazarus' grave.

The first truth was revealed when Jesus said that Lazarus was asleep and that He would wake him (vv. 11-14). His disciples responded, "Lord, if he sleeps, he will get better." Jesus replied, "Lazarus is dead." Saying that He would waken Lazarus, I believe, was His gentle way to teach them that they didn't need to dread death any more than sleep. Because of His power, resurrecting someone from the grave was like waking someone from sleep.

I saw a second truth in Jesus' statement to Martha: "He who believes in me will live, even though he dies; and whoever lives and believes in me will never die" (vv. 25-26). Of course, believers aren't exempt from dying physically, but Jesus promised that they would live eternally. As the resurrection and the life, He will "waken" their bodies someday. His power to do this was demonstrated when He raised Lazarus (vv. 43-44).

When someone we love goes to be with Jesus, these promises give us comfort and assurance.   —JOANIE YODER

Two Daughters

Now when Jesus returned, a crowd welcomed him, for they were all expecting him. Then a man named Jairus, a ruler of the synagogue, came and fell at Jesus' feet, pleading with him to come to his house because his only daughter, a girl of about twelve, was dying. . . .

While Jesus was still speaking, someone came from the house of Jairus, the synagogue ruler. "Your daughter is dead," he said. "Don't bother the teacher any more." Hearing this, Jesus said to Jairus, "Don't be afraid; just believe, and she will be healed."

When he arrived at the house of Jairus, he did not let anyone go in with him except Peter, John and James, and the child's father and mother. Meanwhile, all the people were wailing and mourning for her. "Stop wailing," Jesus said. "She is not dead but asleep."

They laughed at him, knowing that she was dead. But he took her by the hand and said, "My child, get up!" Her spirit returned, and at once she stood up.

—LUKE 8:40–42, 49–55

I had never thought much about Jairus before. Oh, I had heard the story about this synagogue ruler, and I knew he had begged Jesus to come to his house and heal his dying daughter. But I never understood the depth of his sorrow. I never understood how his heart must have shattered in pain when a messenger came to him and announced, "Your daughter is dead."

No, I never comprehended his grief and anguish—until I heard those same words from a police officer who came to our house on June 6, 2002.

Jairus' daughter was twelve, and she died from an illness. Our daughter was seventeen; and it was an auto accident that broke our family's heart.

Jairus' daughter was restored to life by Jesus' touch. My daughter Melissa—though we ache knowing she wasn't healed physically—was healed spiritually by Jesus' sacrifice of love when she trusted Him as Savior early in her life. Now our comfort comes from knowing that her eternal existence with the Lord has already begun.

Two daughters. The same Jesus. Two different results. His loving and compassionate touch is a miracle that can bring peace to grieving hearts—like Jairus', like mine, like yours.

—DAVE BRANON

A Circle of Compassion

Praise be to the God and Father of our Lord Jesus Christ, the Father of compassion and the God of all comfort, who comforts us in all our troubles, so that we can comfort those in any trouble with the comfort we ourselves have received from God.

—2 CORINTHIANS 1:3–4

*F*ollowing the death of our seventeen-year-old daughter in a car accident, each member of our family handled the loss differently. For my wife, among the most helpful sources of comfort were visits from moms who had also lost a child in an accident.

Sue found strength in their stories, and she wanted them to tell her how God had been faithful in their lives, despite the deep sorrow that comes with losing a precious child.

Soon Sue became part of a circle of compassion, a small group of moms who could weep, pray, and seek God's help together. That cadre of grieving moms formed a bond of empathy and hope that provided encouragement in the face of her daily sorrow.

Each person grieves uniquely, yet we all need to share our hearts, our burdens, our questions, and our sadness with someone else. That's why it's vital that we find others with whom to discuss our pain and sorrow.

In our relationship with Christ, we find encouragement, consolation, love, fellowship, affection, and mercy (Philippians 2:1). God comforts us so that we can comfort others (2 Corinthians 1:4). So let's "rejoice with those who rejoice, and weep with those who weep" (Romans 12:15 NKJV). Then others will find a circle of compassion too. —DAVE BRANON

In His Presence

Then I saw a new heaven and a new earth, for the first heaven and the first earth had passed away, and there was no longer any sea. I saw the Holy City, the new Jerusalem, coming down out of heaven from God, prepared as a bride beautifully dressed for her husband. And I heard a loud voice from the throne saying, "Now the dwelling of God is with men, and he will live with them. They will be his people, and God himself will be with them and be their God. He will wipe every tear from their eyes. There will be no more death or mourning or crying or pain, for the old order of things has passed away." —REVELATION 21:1–4

As the congregation around me sang the final verse of "Amazing Grace," I couldn't sing. I found myself instead wiping tears from my eyes as I stared at John Newton's familiar words, "When we've been there 10,000 years, . . . we've no less days to sing God's praise than when we'd first begun."

At that moment I wasn't interested in 10,000 years in heaven. All I could think of was that my seventeen-year-old daughter was already there. Melissa, who just a few months earlier had been looking forward to her senior year of high school, was in heaven. She was already experiencing an eternity that we can only talk and sing about.

When Melissa was killed in a car accident, heaven took on new meaning for our family. Because our bright, beautiful teen had trusted Jesus Christ as her Savior, we knew she was there. As Paul said, "Death is swallowed up in victory" (1 Corinthians 15:54 NKJV). To us, heaven became even more real. We knew that as we talked with God, we were talking to Someone who had our Melissa in His presence.

The reality of heaven is one of the Bible's most glorious truths. It's a real place where our loved ones live in the presence of our great God, forever serving Him and singing His praises—all because of His amazing grace! —DAVE BRANON

Still Trusting

For you created my inmost being;
  you knit me together in my mother's womb.
I praise you because I am fearfully and wonderfully
  made . . .

My frame was not hidden from you
  when I was made in the secret place.
  When I was woven together in the depths of the earth,
your eyes saw my unformed body.
  All the days ordained for me
  were written in your book
  before one of them came to be.

—PSALM 139:13–16

How could this happen? How could God allow our beautiful daughter Melissa to be taken from us in a car accident at age seventeen? And it's not just us. It's also our friends Steve and Robyn, whose daughter Lindsay, Melissa's friend, died nine months earlier. And what about Richard and Leah, whose son Jon—another of Melissa's friends—lies in a gravesite within fifty yards of both Lindsay and Melissa?

How could God allow these three Christian teens to die within sixteen months of each other? And how can we still trust Him?

Unable to comprehend such tragedies, we cling to Psalm 139:16—"All the days ordained for me were written in your book." By God's design, our children had a specific number of days to live, and then He lovingly called them home to their eternal reward. And we find comfort in God's mysterious words, "Precious in the sight of the Lord is the death of his saints" (Psalm 116:15).

The death of those close to us could rob us of our trust in God—taking with it our reason for living. But God's unfathomable plan for the universe and His redemptive work continue, and we must honor our loved ones by holding on to His hand. We don't understand, but we still must trust God as we await the great reunion He has planned for us.

—DAVE BRANON

Ascended!

Now we know that if the earthly tent we live in is destroyed, we have a building from God, an eternal house in heaven, not built by human hands. Meanwhile we groan, longing to be clothed with our heavenly dwelling, because when we are clothed, we will not be found naked. For while we are in this tent, we groan and are burdened, because we do not wish to be unclothed but to be clothed with our heavenly dwelling, so that what is mortal may be swallowed up by life. Now it is God who has made us for this very purpose and has given us the Spirit as a deposit, guaranteeing what is to come.

Therefore we are always confident and know that as long as we are at home in the body we are away from the Lord. We live by faith, not by sight. We are confident, I say, and would prefer to be away from the body and at home with the Lord.

—2 CORINTHIANS 5:1–8

*J*oseph Parker (1830–1902) was a beloved English preacher. When his wife died, he didn't have the customary wording inscribed on her gravestone. Instead of the word *died* followed by the date of her death, he chose the word *ascended*.

Parker found great comfort in being reminded that though his wife's body had been placed in the grave, the "real" Mrs. Parker had been transported to heaven and into the presence of her Savior. When Parker himself died, his friends made sure that his gravestone read: Ascended November 28, 1902.

When a believing loved one dies, or when we ourselves face the process of dying, there's great comfort in the fact that "to be absent from the body" is "to be present with the Lord" (2 Corinthians 5:8 NKJV).

Death for us is not a dark journey into the unknown. It is not a lonely walk into a strange and friendless place. Rather, it is a glorious transition from the trials of earth into the joys of heaven, where we will be reunited with our loved ones in Christ who have gone before. Best of all, we will enjoy the presence of our Lord forever.

Yes, when a believer dies, the body is buried but not the soul. It has ascended! —RICHARD DE HAAN

For Whom the Bell Tolls

But whatever was to my profit I now consider loss for the sake of Christ. What is more, I consider everything a loss compared to the surpassing greatness of knowing Christ Jesus my Lord, for whose sake I have lost all things. I consider them rubbish, that I may gain Christ and be found in him, not having a righteousness of my own that comes from the law, but that which is through faith in Christ—the righteousness that comes from God and is by faith. I want to know Christ and the power of his resurrection and the fellowship of sharing in his sufferings, becoming like him in his death, and so, somehow, to attain to the resurrection from the dead. —PHILIPPIANS 3:7–11

*I*n 17th-century England, church bells tolled out the news of what was taking place in a parish. They announced not only religious services but also weddings and funerals.

So when John Donne, author and dean of St. Paul's Cathedral, lay desperately sick with the plague that was killing people in London by the thousands, he could hear the bells announce death after death. Writing down his thoughts in the devotional diary that became a classic, Donne urged his readers, "Never send to know for whom the bell tolls. It tolls for thee."

How true! The book of Hebrews teaches that we will all face death one day: "It is appointed for men to die once, but after this the judgment" (Hebrews 9:27 NKJV).

But if we are believers in the gospel, news of death does not need to arouse dread. We know, as Paul joyfully assured us, that by His resurrection Jesus broke the power of death and "brought life and immortality to light through the gospel" (2 Timothy 1:10). Death has been "swallowed up in victory" by the Lord Jesus Christ. Its sting is gone (1 Corinthians 15:54–55).

When the bell tolls for the Christian, it announces the good news of Jesus' victory over death.   —VERNON GROUNDS

How God Makes Comforters

Praise be to the God and Father of our Lord Jesus Christ, the Father of compassion and the God of all comfort, who comforts us in all our troubles, so that we can comfort those in any trouble with the comfort we ourselves have received from God. For just as the sufferings of Christ flow over into our lives, so also through Christ our comfort overflows. If we are distressed, it is for your comfort and salvation; if we are comforted, it is for your comfort, which produces in you patient endurance of the same sufferings we suffer. And our hope for you is firm, because we know that just as you share in our sufferings, so also you share in our comfort.

—2 CORINTHIANS 1:3–7

Little wisdom is acquired in days of prosperity and carefree happiness, but what marvelous lessons we learn in the university of pain and tears! We discover that God has a special key of consolation to fit every lock of sorrow. And when we have experienced His comfort, we can best help others.

J. W. Bramhall says, "Sorrow can lead us into one of four lands: the barren land in which we try to escape from it; the broken land in which we sink under it; the bitter land in which we resent it; or the better land in which we bear it and become a blessing to others."

An elderly Chinese philosopher was once approached by a young woman who was grief stricken because of the loss of her only son. "I will be able to help you," he assured her, "if you will bring me some mustard seed; but it must be obtained at a home where there has never been any sorrow." Eagerly the woman started her search. In every place she visited, however, there had been trials and loss of loved ones. Returning, she exclaimed, "How selfish I have been! Sorrow is common to all." "Ah," said the elderly sage, "you have now learned a valuable lesson and acquired a wealth of wisdom which not only has eased your own grief, but also has prepared you to sympathize with others."

If the God of all comfort has consoled you, Christian, and given you fresh perspectives of His grace, don't hoard up that precious treasure. Having experienced His balm of healing, use it to help those by your side who need compassion and understanding.　　　　　　　　　　　　　　　—HENRY BOSCH

Hurt to Heal

Praise be to the God and Father of our Lord Jesus Christ, the Father of compassion and the God of all comfort, who comforts us in all our troubles, so that we can comfort those in any trouble with the comfort we ourselves have received from God. For just as the sufferings of Christ flow over into our lives, so also through Christ our comfort overflows. If we are distressed, it is for your comfort and salvation; if we are comforted, it is for your comfort, which produces in you patient endurance of the same sufferings we suffer. And our hope for you is firm, because we know that just as you share in our sufferings, so also you share in our comfort.

—2 Corinthians 1:3–7

God may allow us to be hurt so that in our healing He may make us healers of others. The apostle Paul declared that God "comforts us in all our troubles, so that we can comfort those in any trouble with the comfort we ourselves have received from God" (2 Corinthians 1:4). Countless numbers of God's people have suffered sickness, hardship, and adversity, which has prepared them to minister to others.

V. Gilbert Beers, a highly respected Christian leader, said that he and his wife learned the meaning of 2 Corinthians 1:4 through the sudden death of their oldest son. They were heartbroken, but as the weeks passed they began to experience God's marvelous healing. Then they found themselves being drawn into the lives of other hurting people. Beers wrote, "We began to discover in succeeding months that we were healing other wounded people as we had never done before."

We need not ask God to wound us through heartbreak, pain, or persecution. Wounds will come. Living in a sinful world, we are bound to experience suffering sooner or later. But we can be assured that God has permitted our pain for our good. Deeply believing this brings us God's comfort, healing, and peace. Through our pain and our experience of His gracious provision, we can become better equipped than ever before to bring comfort and healing to others.

—HERB VANDER LUGT

The Final Tears

On this mountain he will destroy
   the shroud that enfolds all peoples,
the sheet that covers all nations;
   he will swallow up death forever.
The Sovereign Lord will wipe away the tears
   from all faces;
he will remove the disgrace of his people
   from all the earth.
            The Lord has spoken.
In that day they will say,
"Surely this is our God;
   we trusted in him, and he saved us.
This is the Lord, we trusted in him;
   let us rejoice and be glad in his salvation."

—Isaiah 25:7–9

*T*his world has been rightly called "a vale of tears." People everywhere are wiping their eyes because of some frustration, some cherished hope crushed, some loved one snatched from their embrace, or some besetting sin that is bringing sorrow and regret. But praise God there is a better day ahead for the believer. He comes to heaven, as it were, with misty eyes and tear-stained face, only to feel the tender hand of God gently stroking his brow and clearing his beclouded vision with the handkerchief of His eternal comfort. No more sorrow shall distress us over there. When the Savior wipes our eyes we shall have experienced our final tears.

Howard W. Ferrin says,

> God's handkerchief is embroidered with love and tender sympathy, and it is the pierced hand that puts it to the eyes of the weeping ones. God will dry every tear: tears of misfortune and poverty, tears of bereaved affection, tears of doubt and discouragement, tears of pain, tears of fear, tears of neglect, tears of yearning for what cannot now be ours; yes, each tear shall be fully wiped away by Him who knows our every sorrow.

Bereaved and distressed saint, your present grieving shall have an end. "Weeping may endure for a night," but praise the Lord, "joy comes in the morning" (Psalm 30:5 NKJV). In God's bright eternal day, tears will be unknown!

—HENRY BOSCH

Comforted by God

Praise be to the God and Father of our Lord Jesus Christ, the Father of compassion and the God of all comfort, who comforts us in all our troubles, so that we can comfort those in any trouble with the comfort we ourselves have received from God. For just as the sufferings of Christ flow over into our lives, so also through Christ our comfort overflows. —2 CORINTHIANS 1:3–5

How reassuring to know that the Lord is abundantly able to carry us through our night of sorrow! Indeed, He is the "God of all comfort" (2 Corinthians 1:3). Though His ways may distress us at the moment, they are always right and gracious. So, rather than fretting and complaining, we ought to trust and praise Him. What the Lord has planned for us is designed for our good, and Heaven will reveal that He sent nothing to hurt us but only to bless us. As Christians, we should therefore cast all our care upon the Lord, implicitly believing that He is truly concerned about us (1 Peter 5:7).

The story is told of a mother who was trying to calm her fretful little daughter who had climbed up on her lap. Soon the mother's loving embrace and tender caresses quieted the four-year-old's uneasiness. But the mother herself was grieving, for she had just laid to rest her own dear mother, who in days past had been such a spiritual help to her. Looking up, the little girl saw her mother's moist eyes and asked sweetly, "Mama, do you want to be holded too?" Then the mother's tears began to flow freely, and the child hugged her and whispered, "Mama, God will hold you, won't He?" The woman was both chided and consoled. Looking to the Lord in her grief, she found grace and solace.

If you are troubled, turn your problems over to the loving Savior. It's the only way to find peace of mind. Then with the psalmist you too will soon be able to testify: "When anxiety was great within me, your consolation brought joy to my soul" (Psalm 94:19).

—HENRY BOSCH

With Christ in Paradise

Then he said, "Jesus, remember me when you come into your kingdom." Jesus answered him, "I tell you the truth, today you will be with me in paradise."

—LUKE 23:42–43

He who has an ear, let him hear what the Spirit says to the churches. To him who overcomes, I will give the right to eat from the tree of life, which is in the paradise of God.

—REVELATION 2:7

---

*M*issionary David Miner Stern was plunged into grief when God saw fit to take to Himself his precious little daughter. Stern could not seem to get over his great sorrow. He became so depressed that he went daily to the cemetery to mourn by her grave. With his walking stick he would touch the mound of earth that covered the casket. Somehow this seemed to give him a measure of comfort—as though he still had some slight contact with her. His grief was so oppressive that he feared he would have to give up his labors as a missionary.

However, God graciously brought him relief. One day as he stood in the cemetery, he suddenly realized how wrong it was to fix his attention on the dead body of his little daughter. The Holy Spirit impressed on his mind the truth in Luke 23:43, where Jesus said to the dying thief "Today you will be with me in paradise." He began repeating the words "with Christ in paradise" as he walked home. The blessed reality that his daughter was with Jesus increasingly dawned on him. He said to himself, "What more could I ask for my loved one than this?" In the comfort of this thought he was able to resume his duties with joy. Instead of thinking of his daughter in the grave, he visualized her safe in Jesus' presence.

Are you grieving because God has taken a loved one from you? Remind yourself often that those who die in the Lord are with Christ in paradise. —HENRY BOSCH

He Understands

He was despised and rejected by men,
  a man of sorrows, and familiar with suffering.
Like one from whom men hide their faces
  he was despised, and we esteemed him not.

Surely he took up our infirmities
  and carried our sorrows,
yet we considered him stricken by God,
  smitten by him, and afflicted.
But he was pierced for our transgressions,
  he was crushed for our iniquities;
the punishment that brought us peace was upon him,
  and by his wounds we are healed.

—ISAIAH 53:3–5

How comforting it is to know that we have a Savior who can identify with our trials, suffering, and sorrow! Our Lord knew both physical and mental anguish.

Isaiah wrote, "He was despised and rejected by men, a man of sorrows and familiar with grief" (Isaiah 53:3). Jesus knew the suffering caused by being misunderstood. Members of His own family did not understand that He had come to die. He experienced the pain of poverty. He faced strong temptations. He felt the sorrow of losing a good friend to death (John 11).

Gordon Chilvers tells of a grief-stricken mother. The death of a wayward daughter had left her crushed with sorrow. Although her pastor and friends did all they could to comfort her, her grief was so heavy that she couldn't cry. Then a woman came to see her who had experienced an identical loss. She sat down beside the sorrowing mother and lovingly placed an arm around her. With her face close to the face of the grieving woman, she wept. Soon the bereaved mother began to weep and relief came at last. That woman could sympathize because she had known the same sorrow.

We have One who has experienced deep suffering. Tell Him about your pain and draw on His strength. He understands and cares. —PAUL VAN GORDER

When Jesus Grieved

The king [Herod] . . . had John beheaded in the prison. . . . John's disciples came and took his body and buried it. Then they went and told Jesus.

When Jesus heard what had happened, he withdrew by boat privately to a solitary place. Hearing of this, the crowds followed him on foot from the towns. When Jesus landed and saw a large crowd, he had compassion on them and healed their sick.

—MATTHEW 14:9, 12–14

*M*any years ago, a backcountry woman in Florida received news that her son had been killed in the war. Shortly thereafter, she was seen hoeing in her garden.

"It just isn't fitting," chided a neighbor who thought it was inappropriate to be gardening instead of grieving.

"Friend," said Effie Mae, "I know you mean well, but Jim rejoiced to see green things growing because it meant that his mother and the young ones would be eating. This is his hoe, and when I'm hoeing I can almost feel his big, strong hands under mine and hear his voice saying, 'That's good, Mom, that's good.' Working is the only headstone I can give him."

Jesus also suffered the pain of grief when He was told of the death of John the Baptist, but it didn't deter Him from His work. After a brief period of solitude (Matthew 14:13), His great compassion led Him to heal the sick and to feed the multitude of 5,000.

Is your heart broken today? Does life seem empty? Do you feel like giving up? There is hope in the Master's example. Take up whatever duties lie before you. Dedicate them to God. Refuse the luxury of self-pity. Do something to lift the burdens of others. Remember how Jesus handled His sorrow; He'll strengthen you to do the same.   —DENNIS DE HAAN

Comfort for Today

Praise be to the God and Father of our Lord Jesus Christ! In his great mercy he has given us new birth into a living hope through the resurrection of Jesus Christ from the dead, and into an inheritance that can never perish, spoil or fade—kept in heaven for you, who through faith are shielded by God's power until the coming of the salvation that is ready to be revealed in the last time. In this you greatly rejoice, though now for a little while you may have had to suffer grief in all kinds of trials. These have come so that your faith—of greater worth than gold, which perishes even though refined by fire—may be proved genuine and may result in praise, glory and honor when Jesus Christ is revealed. Though you have not seen him, you love him; and even though you do not see him now, you believe in him and are filled with an inexpressible and glorious joy, for you are receiving the goal of your faith, the salvation of your souls. —1 PETER 1:3–9

Over the last fifty years I have often reminded bereaved people of the wonderful truth that a glorious resurrection awaits all who believe on Jesus Christ. But sometimes, grieving people are so overwhelmed with their loss that they cannot rejoice in the prospect of a far-off-in-the-future reunion.

In John 11, we read about Martha's struggle between her feelings and what she knew to be true. She was grieving because her brother Lazarus had died. When Jesus spoke with her, she told Him that she believed in a future day of resurrection. But then Jesus took her a step further and helped her to find comfort by focusing on Him rather than just on a future event. He declared, "I am the resurrection and the life" (v. 25). This led her to confess her faith in Him (v. 27). Her new focus on Him must have helped her because she then went to her sister Mary and told her to come to Jesus (v. 28).

It's wonderful to know that because Jesus died for our sins and rose from the grave we can look forward to a day of resurrection. But it's even more comforting to know and trust the One who is the resurrection and the life. He is present with us today to comfort, reassure, and strengthen us through all our circumstances (Matthew 28:20).   —HERB VANDER LUGT

Snapshots of Heaven

Brothers, we do not want you to be ignorant about those who fall asleep, or to grieve like the rest of men, who have no hope. We believe that Jesus died and rose again and so we believe that God will bring with Jesus those who have fallen asleep in him. According to the Lord's own word, we tell you that we who are still alive, who are left till the coming of the Lord, will certainly not precede those who have fallen asleep. For the Lord himself will come down from heaven, with a loud command, with the voice of the archangel and with the trumpet call of God, and the dead in Christ will rise first. After that, we who are still alive and are left will be caught up together with them in the clouds to meet the Lord in the air. And so we will be with the Lord forever. Therefore encourage each other with these words.

—I Thessalonians 4:13–18

I asked my ten-year-old son, Steve, "Why do you want to go to heaven?" I expected to hear something about streets of gold or not having to go to school or something similar. Instead, he said, "Because I want to see Grandpa."

It's been several years since my dad, Steve's grandpa, went to be with the Lord. But I don't think time will ever diminish how much Steve admires and misses his World War II veteran grandfather. That's why the fact that Steve will see him again in heaven is so important to him.

The prospect of heaven is one of the most comforting truths in the Bible. Not only can we find hope in knowing that we will someday be in Jesus' presence, but we can also anticipate seeing loved ones who are waiting for us on the other side (1 Thessalonians 4:14,17).

Imagine a grieving widow who has the assurance of being reunited with her husband of fifty years. Imagine sorrowing parents knowing that their child who succumbed to disease will be reunited with them. What a wonderful hope!

The promise of reunion in heaven gives us a glimpse of what our eternal home will be like. The prospect of seeing the people we love gives us snapshots of heaven in an album of hope.

—DAVE BRANON

When Jesus Is Glad

Now we know that if the earthly tent we live in is destroyed, we have a building from God, an eternal house in heaven, not built by human hands. . . . Therefore we are always confident and know that as long as we are at home in the body we are away from the Lord. We live by faith, not by sight. We are confident, I say, and would prefer to be away from the body and at home with the Lord. So we make it our goal to please him, whether we are at home in the body or away from it. For we must all appear before the judgment seat of Christ, that each one may receive what is due him for the things done while in the body, whether good or bad. —2 CORINTHIANS 5:1, 6–10

A woman wrote to RBC Ministries about her mother who went home to be with the Lord. She was much loved and a blessing to everyone who met her. The writer shared what her seven-year-old son said about the home going of his grandmother. Expressing his great love and admiration for her, he remarked with childish glee, "I'll bet Jesus was glad to see Grandma!"

I heartily agree. I'm sure the Lord welcomes home all whom He has redeemed. When we think about the death of a Christian, our minds are usually taken up with the joy that a believer must experience when he first sees the One who saved him. What a thrill to behold Christ for the first time! Yes, we'll be happy to see Christ. But He who loved the church so much that He gave His life for her surely rejoices each time one of His redeemed ones arrives home. I'm confident that when we who have trusted Him as Savior pass through the gates of glory, our Redeemer will find great satisfaction in receiving us into His presence.

So, believer, whether you are facing death yourself or are grieving over the loss of a loved one, think of that boy's words, "I'll bet Jesus was glad to see Grandma." I'm sure He will be glad to see you too!   —RICHARD DE HAAN

No Grieving Allowed

While they were stoning him, Stephen prayed, "Lord Jesus, receive my spirit." Then he fell on his knees and cried out, "Lord, do not hold this sin against them." When he had said this, he fell asleep. . . . Godly men buried Stephen and mourned deeply for him.

—ACTS 7:59–60; 8:2

Rejoice with those who rejoice; mourn with those who mourn.

—ROMANS 12:15

The American Hospice Foundation says that bereaved people tend to keep their grieving a secret in the workplace. Many of us have grown up with the idea that sorrow should be overcome quickly. What often happens is that we deny our pain, bottle it up inside, and try to go it alone. A sign that reads "No Grieving Allowed" might as well be posted on the walls at work.

Unfortunately, this same dangerous attitude can invade our homes and communities of faith as well. Grieving presents a dilemma for many Christians. When we feel the deep pain of loss, we often hide it, believing we should be outwardly joyful no matter what has happened. But notice the words of Acts 8:2. Luke wrote that after Stephen was stoned to death by an angry mob, godly men buried him and "mourned deeply for him." Godly men crying and mourning deeply may seem contradictory to some, but the Bible states it plainly in all its emotional impact.

The Lord never asks us to ignore the pain in our hearts. Instead, He calls us to "weep with those who weep" (Romans 12:15 NKJV). We are to love and support one another as we move together through the process of grieving.

—DAVID MCCASLAND

Outside the Family Circle

Near the cross of Jesus stood his mother, his mother's sister, Mary the wife of Clopas, and Mary Magdalene. When Jesus saw his mother there, and the disciple whom he loved standing nearby, he said to his mother, "Dear woman, here is your son," and to the disciple, "Here is your mother." From that time on, this disciple took her into his home. —JOHN 19:25–27

When Jesus saw His mother from the cross, His heart went out to her. He knew that her hurt was deeper than that of anyone else there, and He gave her special attention.

The pain of parents when they see a son or daughter suffer and die is almost beyond description. I have seen this time and time again when ministering to grieving parents. I suffer with them, but all the while I know that my hurt doesn't compare with what I would be feeling if the suffering and dying person were my son, daughter, or grandchild.

This sometimes troubles me. Although I want to be a genuinely caring person, and I want to "weep with those who weep," I also realize that I can't grieve as deeply as the family members do. But just because I'm outside the family doesn't give me an excuse to be uncaring.

God wants us to share in the sorrows of others (Romans 12:15). Instead of ignoring their pain, we should be sharing in it by earnest prayer, kind words, and loving deeds.

Thank God for family ties. It's natural to have a deep sense of loss when someone close to us dies. But we should also look for ways to enter into the sorrows of others who are grieving.

—HERB VANDER LUGT

Ministry of Remembering

Love must be sincere. Hate what is evil; cling to what is good. Be devoted to one another in brotherly love. Honor one another above yourselves. Never be lacking in zeal, but keep your spiritual fervor, serving the Lord. Be joyful in hope, patient in affliction, faithful in prayer. Share with God's people who are in need. Practice hospitality.

Bless those who persecute you; bless and do not curse. Rejoice with those who rejoice; mourn with those who mourn.

—ROMANS 12:9–15

*T*he holidays can be a difficult time for people who are grieving. Friends may be reluctant to mention the name of someone who has died, fearing that it will cause unnecessary pain. But during those few weeks, friends or family members may need you to talk openly with them about the person they have lost. Call it the "ministry of remembering."

A chaplain at a Connecticut hospital says, "When you've experienced the loss through death of a spouse, child, or parent, it hurts terribly. And when people don't want to use their names or refer to the death, it's like losing that person all over again."

Bereaved people ache for opportunities to talk about their loved ones, whether the person died last week or many years ago. Even though remembering may bring tears, it can also produce emotional release and even joy.

Tucked into a series of commands in Romans 12, we find these words: "Rejoice with those who rejoice; mourn with those who mourn" (v. 15). Sharing a time of remembering with a hurting friend may help to ease a heavy burden.

If someone comes to mind, don't put it off. Pray, make the phone call, stop by for a visit, or invite the friend to lunch. It may be the most important thing you do today.

—David McCasland

About the Authors

Henry Bosch served as the first editor of the daily devotional booklet that became *Our Daily Bread* (ODB) and contributed many of the earliest articles. He was also one of the singers on the Radio Bible Class live broadcast.

Dave Branon has done freelance writing for many years and has published more than thirteen books. Dave taught English and coached basketball and baseball at the high school level before coming to RBC Ministries (RBC), where he is now the Managing Editor of *Sports Spectrum* magazine.

Dennis De Haan is a nephew of RBC founder Dr. M. R. De Haan. He pastored two churches in Iowa and Michigan before joining the RBC staff in 1971. He served as Associate Editor of ODB from 1973 until 1982 and then as Editor until June 1995. Now retired, Dennis continues editing for ODB on a part-time basis.

Mart De Haan is the grandson of RBC founder, Dr. M. R. De Haan, and the son of former president, Richard W. De Haan. Having served at RBC for over thirty years, Mart is heard regularly on the *Discover the Word* radio program and seen on *Day of Discovery* television. Mart is also a contributing writer for ODB, the Discovery Series Bible study booklets, and a monthly column on timely issues called "Been Thinking About."

Richard De Haan was President of RBC Ministries and teacher on RBC programs for twenty years. He was the son of RBC founder

Dr. M. R. De Haan and wrote a number of full-length books and study booklets for RBC. Often called "the encourager," Richard was committed to faithfulness to God's Word and to integrity as a ministry. His favorite expression was "Trust in God and do the right." Richard went to be with the Lord in 2002.

Dave Egner is now retired from RBC. He was (until June 2002) Managing Editor of *Campus Journal*. He has written Discovery Series study booklets and articles for a variety of publications. Dave taught English and writing for ten years at Grand Rapids Baptist College (now Cornerstone University) before coming to RBC.

Vernon Grounds, Chancellor of Denver Seminary, has had an extensive preaching, teaching, and counseling ministry and was president of Denver Seminary. In addition to writing articles for ODB, he has also written many books and magazine articles.

David McCasland researches and helps develop biographical documentaries for *Day of Discovery* television, in addition to writing ODB articles. His books include the award-winning biography *Oswald Chambers: Abandoned to God,* a compilation of *The Complete Works of Oswald Chambers*, and *Pure Gold,* a biography of Eric Liddell.

Paul Van Gorder began writing regularly for ODB in 1969 and continued until 1992. He also served as associate Bible teacher for the *Day of Discovery* television program and traveled extensively as a speaker for Radio Bible Class. He and his wife now live in retirement in South Carolina.

Herb Vander Lugt is Senior Research Editor for RBC Ministries and has been at RBC since 1966. In addition to ODB articles, he also writes Discovery Series booklets and reviews all study and devotional materials. Herb has pastored six churches and since retiring from the pastorate in 1989 has held three interim pastor positions.

Joanie Yoder, a favorite among ODB readers, went home to be with her Savior in 2004. She and her husband established a Christian rehabilitation center for drug addicts in England many years ago. Widowed in 1982, she learned to rely on the Lord's help and strength. She wrote with hope about true dependence on God and His life-changing power.